# BECAUSE

Bible study for beginners by
Michele Zimmerman

BECAUSE

All rights reserved. No part of this book may be reproduced, stored in a retrieval system or transmitted in any form or by any means- electronic, mechanical, digital, photocopy, recording, or any other without the prior permission of the author. Unless otherwise identified, all Scripture quotations in this publication are taken from the Holy Bible, New King James Version Copyright ©1979,1980,1982 by Thomas Nelson Inc publishers

Verses marked Contemporary English Version CEV are taken from the Holy Bible,Contemporary English Version. Copyright ©1991,1992,1995 by American Bible Society. Used by Permission

Scripture taken from the Holy Bible,New Testament International Version (NIV)Copyright ©1973, 1978, 1984 by International Bible Society.Used by permission of Zondervan Publishing House

Copyright © 2020 Michele Zimmerman

ISBN:978-1-7342700-2-0

# BECAUSE
## BIBLE STUDY FOR BEGINNERS

BECAUSE

BECAUSE

# CONTENTS

|    | Acknowledgments | vii |
|----|-----------------|-----|
|    | Intro | ix |
| 1  | Bible Basics | 3 |
| 2  | The Blood | 15 |
| 3  | Offerings | 25 |
| 4  | The Feasts | 33 |
| 5  | Unity | 43 |
| 6  | Adopted | 55 |
| 7  | Prayer | 63 |
| 8  | Intercession and Fasting | 73 |
| 9  | Spiritual Understanding | 81 |
| 10 | Discipleship and The Great Commission | 91 |

BECAUSE

# ACKNOWLEDGMENTS

Special Recognition to Pastor Rick Rampersad and Marla Hall for volunteering your wise counsel and valuable feedback on this project. Thank you for your enduring patience through all the edits and rewrites. Most of all, thank you for your encouragement and prayer through this process. I appreciate you and your families so very much.

For you, the reader- thank you for sojourning with me. My prayer for you is that you will grow more curious in the study of scripture and will understand beyond any shadow of doubt that God's word is true, living, full of power and effective for equipping you for your purpose.

Seek Him and He will be found.

Because it is written!

BECAUSE

## INTRO

Have you ever asked "Why?" and received the response, "Because I said so!" with absolutely no other explanation? Growing up that was a typical response from my parents and my babysitter. Granted, it was mostly out of their frustration from me asking it so often. I'll admit sometimes I asked "why?" for no other reason except to get a reaction, especially out of the sitter. Thankfully, God redeemed my need to know. Now many years later, in my profession, it's literally my job to find written support for "why" something was done.

As a Christian I have asked God "why?" many times, and in case you are wondering, yes, sometimes it was out of my own frustration and yes, sometimes to get His reaction. Most of all, I want to know Him more, to know about Him, and to be with Him, in His presence. That's the reaction I am settled on. His word is life giving to me. When others share the same desire to learn, grow and understand with me, it's icing on the cake. For that reason I am so happy you have decided to pick up this study and join me.

I love Jesus and I believe the Bible is the inspired, infallible, and inerrant word of God.

The history of the Bible is remarkable, it's written by approximately 40 authors from a variety of socioeconomic backgrounds, each bringing their own personality and perspective over the course of 1500 years.

Both the Old and New Testament are full of stories of men and women who by human standards failed miserably, but God used them in a powerful way. The ancient priests of the Old Testament were responsible for the preservation of the law spoken through Moses, and scribes meticulously copied those scripture writings. After Jesus's death, resurrection and ascension into heaven, many Christians willingly endured persecution, imprisonment and death. Many were martyred for their belief.

The Apostle Paul *(Roman/Latin name)*, also called Saul *(Hebrew name)*, is one of these men. He is known as one of the most influential writers of all time. Many of our New Testament writings come from his hand; however, Paul didn't start out as a Christian. He whole heartedly believed Christianity was a danger to Judaism, and he hated anything that had to do with Christian beliefs. He was a Pharisee and a student of the holy scriptures who studied under the best Rabbi's and meticulously followed the law of Moses. Paul imprisoned and persecuted Christians without remorse. The book of Acts tells us he was present when Stephen, one of the early church deacons was stoned to death (Acts 7:54-56). Saul was on his way to arrest more Christians when Jesus stopped him in his tracks and changed his life forever (Acts 9:1-19)

Acts 9:20 goes on to tell us that Paul immediately preached Christ in the synagogues, proclaiming that Jesus is the son of God. This didn't go over so well with many of the Jews. They, in turn, plotted to kill him (Acts 9:23).

Believers were scattered throughout the land to avoid persecution. Moving to cities like Jerusalem, Antioch, Ephesus and Rome, they formed churches wherever they went. Paul wrote many encouraging letters to these early churches because he understood from experience, both as perpetrator and prisoner, that sharing the gospel came with great cost. He considered it an honor and privilege to be persecuted even unto death because of the cross of Jesus. Biblical scholars believe that Paul's letters were not written until approximately 20 years after Jesus death and resurrection.

Prior to Paul's writing and teaching, the Gospel message was spread by word of mouth from actual eyewitness or historians who personally interviewed these witnesses. (See Luke 24:46-53)

## **Read 1 Corinthians 15:1-6**

Biblical scholars believe 1 Corinthians 3-5 to be a creed that began circulating as early as two years after Jesus's death and resurrection, while other scholars believe it was between 2-7 years. The actual timing isn't as important as the importance of the message found in these words:

- Christ died for our sins
- Christ was buried
- Christ rose again
- He was seen
- He will return for us

That's the Gospel! That's why we study scripture!

A creed is defined as a set of beliefs that guide one's actions. In most cases creeds were easily memorized, understood, and able to be passed down from generation to generation. For the early church a creed was more than just doctrine. Creeds were personal convictions to live by and die for.

As we journey together through BECAUSE, we'll be looking at some basics for how to study the Bible and deepen our relationship with the Lord. Scripture tells us in Proverbs 2:2-5 *"Tune your ears to wisdom, and concentrate on understanding! Cry out for insight, and ask for understanding, search for them as you would for silver; seek them like hidden treasures. Then you will understand what it means to fear the Lord and you will gain knowledge.*

It's okay to ask God why, He actually encourages it. My hope is that you become more comfortable asking those "why" questions and build your confidence for discipling those around you.

Unless otherwise specified, the scripture translation I use is the New King James Version; however, you can use a translation of your own choosing. Feel free to use more than one.

**In addition to your Bible you may find it helpful to have the following at your fingertips:**

- Bible Commentary
- Bible Dictionary
- Strong's Bible Concordance
- Bible Atlas
- Journal or notebook
- Pen or pencil
- Highlighter

**NOTES:**

# BECAUSE

# CHAPTER 1

# BIBLE BASICS

Our Christian Bible is divided into two sections, the Old Testament contains 39 books and the New Testament contains 27 books.

## **OLD TESTAMENT(and its history):**

The Hebrew Bible and our Old Testament share the same books, although they are arranged differently. Ancient scribes meticulously copied the original text and painstakingly preserved it for generations to come. Ancient versions of scripture have been found in many languages including Greek, Hebrew, Aramaic and Latin. For this reason, it's important to understand the original text in which a word is used to gain a better understanding of its meaning. We have many versions of the Bible due to the different manuscripts found, and the changes in our English language throughout centuries. In the Hebrew culture, the first 5 books of the Old Testament (Genesis, Exodus, Leviticus, Numbers, and Deuteronomy) are known as the Torah. In them we find the law God gave to Moses, otherwise known as "The Mosaic Law" or simply "The Law." This same group of books is known as the Greek "Pentateuch."

The "Mishnah" is the categorized, written record of the oral law in Judaism. Over the course of 400 years the Mishnah expanded into the "Talmud" which is a record of interpretations of the Mishnah by hundreds of Rabbi's. This became the foundation for rebuilding the Jewish lifestyle and traditions while in exile and passed down through generations.

"The Law" defines ceremonial cleansing, tithing, offerings, feasts, and other important insights into culture during that time period. We will explore these cultures and traditions more in the chapters ahead. I will be highlighting the foreshadowing of Jesus within these cultures and traditions.

## **NEW TESTAMENT and its History:**

The New Testament is the fulfillment of the Old, as it displays the life, death, resurrection and purpose of Jesus Christ. Through the use of textual criticism *(fancy talk for discovering the origin of a word)*, Biblical scholars have noted that over 5000 Greek, 8000 Latin, and many more manuscripts have been discovered in other languages. These manuscripts have not only spanned different time periods but also different regions of the world. Although there have been minor variations due to hand script through the centuries, each one is attesting to the integrity of the New Testament. The differences do not take away from the meaning of the text. Because the variations can be identified, we have assurance that none of them change the core of the Biblical meaning. If you have a study Bible you will likely see these variations in the footnote sections indicated by *NU-text* (Alexandrian or Egyptian) and *M-text* (Greek).

The 27 books of the New Testament are arranged into categories:

- *The Gospels*
- *The Acts of the Apostles*
- *Paul's Epistles*
- *General letters*
- *Revelation*

## HOW TO READ THE BIBLE

Context is of the utmost importance when it comes to our understanding of scripture, and it's imperative we understand the following:

- Author-*who wrote it?*
- Audience- *who did they write to?*
- Culture of the time-*why did they write it and what was going on at the time it was written?*
- How it applies to us today- *what can we learn from it?*

It's also important to pay attention to context cue words such as:
- If
- And
- But
- Therefore

2 Timothy 3:16-17 tells us that all scripture is given by the inspiration of God and that it is beneficial for us because it gives us instruction for everything we may encounter, so that we will be equipped to do what God has for us to do.

Because scripture is given by the inspiration of God it's important we understand what it is He has to say to us and why. Memorizing Scripture is good, but if we only memorize the words without the context, we can potentially miss the importance of why it was spoken in the first place.

2 Timothy 2:15 tells us, *Be diligent to present yourself approved to God, a worker who does not need to be ashamed, rightly dividing the word of truth.*

Rightly dividing the word of truth is simply cutting it straight, not adding to it and not taking away from it but rather seeking to understand it within the context it was intended.

It's beneficial for our spiritual growth that we develop a daily practice of speaking to God and listening for Him to speak to us through His word. We must incline our ears to listen. (Proverbs 4:20)

**CONTEXT EXERCISE**

In the space below the verses write out what you think they mean.

*Deuteronomy 28:13*
*"And the Lord will make you the head and not the tail; you shall be above only and not beneath…"*

*Isaiah 53:5*
"But He was wounded for our transgressions; he was bruised for our iniquities, the chastisement for our peace was upon Him, And by His stripes we are healed."

*Jeremiah 29:11*
"For I know the thoughts I think toward you, says the Lord… to give you a hope and future."

*Luke 6:38*
"Give, and it will be given to you: good measure, pressed down, shaken together, and running over will be put into your bosom. For with the same measure that you use, it will be measured back to you."

## **Rightly Dividing**

Now, let's "rightly divide" the word by reading it with context from the surrounding verses.

- Read Deuteronomy 28:1-14
- Read Isaiah 53:1-12
- Jeremiah 29:1-14
- Read Luke 6:17-38

Now that you have context around these verses, answer the questions following the example given.

***Example:*** Deuteronomy 28:1-14

- Who is speaking?
    *Moses*
- Whom is he speaking to?
    *The Israelites*
- What's happening in this time period?
    *Moses is giving the Israelites the low down on the blessings tied to their obedience of God's commandments.*
- In the example I gave of 28:13 part of the verse is missing. Write out the verse in its entirety.
    *"And the Lord will make you the head and not the tail; you shall be above only and not beneath if you heed the commandments of the Lord your God, which I command you today, and are careful to observe them."*
- What is the take away?
    *Heeding and observing the commandments is key*

## Isaiah 53:1-12

Who is the author?

To whom is he writing?

Who is Isaiah prophesying about?

What is he prophesying?

Define iniquity:

Define transgressions:

Define chastisement:

What kind of healing is the context referring to?

## Jeremiah 29:1-14

Who is the author?

To Whom is he writing?

What is happening in this time period?

Who is speaking in verse 10-14?

Did your understanding of Jeremiah 29:11 change after you read it in context?

## Luke 6:17-38

Who is speaking?

To whom is He speaking?

BECAUSE

What is happening in this time period?

What is to be given with good measure?

Did your understanding of verse 38 change when you read it in context with the other verses?

I recently heard someone quip "if you take the text out of context you get "con"ned every time." It's true though, if we don't have the right context we can be misled into believing something that's not completely true.

**NOTES:**

BECAUSE

# CHAPTER 2

# THE BLOOD

Salvation is defined as preservation or deliverance from harm, ruin or loss. For Christians, salvation means being delivered or redeemed from the penalty or consequence of sin (which is eternal separation from God.) Ultimately, it is only through the blood of Jesus that redemption comes.

In the Old Testament writings, long before the birth of Jesus we find God's plan for redemption the moment Adam and Eve sinned.

**<u>Read Genesis 3:1-13</u>**

When Adam was created by God, he was formed from dust off the ground, he was without sin. God, Himself, breathed life into Adam (Genesis 2:7). However; when Adam allowed sin to enter his life, he was separated from God, and his sin was then passed down through his bloodline. Adam and Eve could not stay in the Garden of Eden because God could not allow them to live forever in total separation from Him. When there was no sin, there was no separation but now that sin had entered the world there had to be a reconciliation of God to humankind. There had to be a blood sacrifice to repair and make amends for that which was broken.

Sin always brings consequences.

## **Read Genesis 3:14-21**

In the space below write out the consequences for each individual involved.

Satan:

Eve:

Adam:

## Read Genesis 4:1-5

Write below the things that stand out to you in these verses?


We see two different offerings from these two sons of Adam and Eve. The differences in these offerings reveal how we should approach God.

1) What was the offering Cain brought?


2) What was the offering Abel brought?


We don't have much detail as to why God respected Abel and accepted his offering but didn't respect Cain or his offering. What we do see is Cain's angry defiance resulting in Abel's bloodshed. A principle takeaway from this is to remember that God looks at the motivations of our heart, and our desire should be to present our very best to Him.

    A few chapters later in Genesis we read the story of Noah and the ark (Genesis 6-9). In chapter 8, after the flood waters have subsided and Noah and his family exit the ark, Noah builds an altar to the Lord and offers burnt offerings on the altar.

**Read Genesis 8:20-22**

In the space provided below, write out what verse 21 says about Noah's sacrifice.

What does the Lord say specifically in regard to the ground?

**Read Leviticus 17:11**

Where is the life of the flesh?

What makes atonement for the soul?

Science has proven the chemical makeup of blood carries life through the blood cells of the father and mother. Our blood type is determined genetically. Since blood is significant because it represents life, it makes sense that being redeemed by the blood of

Jesus gives us *new* life. We are born again because of **His** blood.

When we read through the Old Testament, we see offerings and sacrifices were regularly practiced. They were used to restore the broken relationship between God and man. Offerings were offered for forgiveness of sins and to show honor and respect to God.

Read Exodus 24:1-8 and answer the questions in the space provided:

v3) What did the Israelites proclaim they would do?


v4) What did Moses do?


v5) Whom did Moses send out to offer sacrifices and peace offerings to God?


v6) What did Moses do with the blood?


v7) What book did Moses read out of?

v7) What was the Israelites response?

v8) What did Moses do with the blood?

v8) Who were the parties involved in the covenant?

This was a covenant sealed by blood and the spoken words of the people.

Read Mark 15:13-14 and Matthew 27:24-25, write out what stands out to you and discuss it with your group.

In ancient days, crucifixion was a form of capital punishment. Criminals were tied or nailed to a cross and left to die. Suffocation would ensue as the weight of the body would weaken, making breathing more difficult. It was the cruelest manner of execution, slow and painful.

As you begin to study God's word, you will find that several Old Testament scriptures foreshadow, or point toward the future of, the death of Jesus as it's written in the New Testament.

## Read Numbers 21:4-9

What was the sin of the Israelites?

What did Moses do? What did God tell Moses to do?

What was the result?

## Read John 3:1-21

What was the question Nicodemus asked Jesus?

In verses 14-15 what did Jesus say needed to happen for someone to be born again?

Read Psalm 22:14-18, Isaiah 53:1-2 and John 19:1-37. Discuss with your group the similarities you find.

## Read Romans 5: 8-11

How did God demonstrate His love for us?

What does justification do for us?

What does it mean to be reconciled?

Jesus; the Anointed One's, death on the cross bridges the gap between us and our heavenly Father.

Truly, "the message of the cross is foolishness to those who are perishing, but to us who are being saved, it is the power of God (1 Corinthians 1:18)"

The only way to salvation is through the blood stained cross. Because of Jesus' blood, we are fully justified, fully forgiven and fully made whole!

**NOTES:**

BECAUSE

# CHAPTER 3

# OFFERINGS

Prior to the cross, offerings and animal sacrifices had to be made to atone for sin. The first animal sacrifice was given by God Himself, when he provided tunics of skin to cover Adam and Eve's nakedness (Genesis 3:21).

In the book of Leviticus, we see five key offerings the Israelites made unto the Lord. Each offering was significant and was to be offered in a specific way. Some of these offerings were voluntary, some mandatory, some frequent, some annual, but all had a very deep meaning. They were divided among God, the Priests, and in some cases, the giver.

Leviticus 1: 1-3
*Now the Lord called to Moses, and spoke to him from the tabernacle of meeting, saying "speak to the children of Israel, and say to them: When any one of you brings an offering to the Lord, you shall bring your offering of the livestock of the herd and of the flock. If his offering is a burnt sacrifice of the herd, let him offer a male without blemish, he shall offer it of his own free will at the door of the tabernacle of meeting before the Lord."*

BECAUSE

The original Hebrew word for sacrifice -"zebach"- means to give up something close to your heart to have a relationship with God. In other words; to "come closer", "draw near", or "be holy." We understand it's a sacrifice to give up something we want for a better outcome later, but imagine giving up something crucial to our very livelihood.

During ancient times, in a purely agricultural environment, an unblemished animal, or produce from their fields held great value. This offering would have been a sacrifice in more ways than one. Oxen, camels, mules, donkeys, and cows were used as pack animals to navigate through the countryside and plow land for crops. Sheep and goats were used for clothing as well as food and drink. Pigeons and chickens were also used for food.

The Israelites had to be self-sustaining in their agricultural society. There was a strong dependency on everything they owned because it was essential to their personal livelihood and survival. This was not just for the humans, but the animals as well, because animals would likely consume grain, fruits and vegetables grown on the land.

God wanted his people to give cheerfully, of their own free will, with an attitude of submission and repentance, not out of compulsion, and by doing so, they demonstrated their sincerity in wanting to restore their relationship with God. Their sacrifice of giving their best to the Lord was an act of worship to Him. Leviticus 1:13 says it was "a sweet aroma to the Lord."

It's evident that there is perfect order to everything God does. These offerings foreshadowed the ultimate penalty paid through Christ Jesus.

Read the scriptures and answer the questions regarding offerings.

## 1. Burnt offering [Leviticus 1:1-17; Leviticus 6:9-13]

Was the burnt offering required or voluntary?

What was the purpose of the burnt offering?

What made the burnt offering significant?

### *Burnt offering is complete in Jesus:*
*Ephesians 5:2: "And walk in love, as Christ has also loved us and given Himself for us, an offering and a sacrifice to God for a sweet smelling aroma."*

## 2. Grain offering [Leviticus 2:1; Leviticus 6:14-23]

Was the grain offering required or voluntary?

What was the purpose of the grain offering?

What made the grain offering significant?

### *Grain offering is complete in Jesus:*
*John 6:35: And Jesus said to them, "I am the bread of life. He who comes to Me shall never hunger, and He who believes in Me shall never thirst"*

## 3. Peace offering [Leviticus 3:1-17; Leviticus 7:11-20]

Was the peace offering required or voluntary?

What was the purpose of the peace offering?

What made the peace offering significant?

## *Peace offering is complete in Jesus:*
*Romans 5:1: Therefore having been justified by faith we have peace with God through our Lord Jesus Christ*

The Peace offering is also known as the fellowship offering, this was divided among God, the Priests and the giver.

## 4. Sin offering [Leviticus 4:1-35; Leviticus 6:25-30]

Was the sin offering required or voluntary?

What was the purpose of the sin offering?

What made the sin offering significant?

## *Sin offering is complete in Jesus:*
*2 Corinthians 5:21: For He made Him who knew no sin to be sin for us, that we might become the righteousness of God in Him.*

## 5. Trespass offering [Leviticus 5: 1-13; Leviticus 7:1-7]

Was the trespass offering required or voluntary?

What was the purpose of the trespass offering?

What made the trespass offering significant?

### *Trespass offering is complete in Jesus:*
*Hebrews 9:15 And for this reason He is the mediator of the new covenant, by means of death, for the redemption of the transgressions under the first covenant, that those who are called may receive the promise of the eternal inheritance*

Jesus made reparations for us once and for all, restoring our fellowship with Father God and with one another.

## 6. Of all of the offerings, which one is the most holy?

## Romans 3:23-26

*For all have sinned and fall short of the glory of God, being justified freely by His grace through the redemption that is in Christ Jesus, whom God set forth as a propitiation by His blood, through faith, to demonstrate His righteousness, because in His forbearance God had passed over the sins that were previously committed, to demonstrate at the present time His righteousness, that He might be just and the justifier of the one who has faith in Jesus.*

Jesus, the spotless lamb, was the fulfillment of the sacrificial system. He willingly laid down His life for us, in order that our relationship with God could be completely restored. Through Him, the consequences of sin were taken away once and for all.

BECAUSE

# CHAPTER 4

# THE FEASTS

Just as we saw God's perfect order for offerings and sacrifices, we will also see His perfect order for feasts, festivals and other traditions. He made a declaration for the Nation of Israel to celebrate sacred feasts. These served as a reminder to His children, of not only His faithfulness, but also for remembrance of how He walked alongside them throughout history. Many of these feasts are still celebrated today within the Jewish community. Each feast emphasizes the importance of unity, sacrifices, offerings and corporate worship.

    The message of the Gospel and anticipation of the coming of Christ the Redeemer is foreshadowed all throughout the Old Testament. Interestingly, there is a parallel seen within these feasts; to the life, death, resurrection, and second coming of Christ. These parallels serve as directional pointers to His final work with redemption, atonement, and forgiveness of sins.
**Read Leviticus 23:1-44**

## SABBATH (v3)

Sabbath, although not a feast, is a Jewish tradition celebrated once a week from Friday evening sundown until Saturday evening sundown. It is a day of solemn rest, meaning no work is to be done. We find the first Sabbath was observed by God when He rested on the 7th day of creation (Genesis 2:2-3).

**New Testament Parallel:**
Jesus rested in the tomb on the seventh day, the day of Sabbath (Mark 15:42-16:12).

## PASSOVER (v5)

This was a week-long feast that reminded the people of God's deliverance. The first passover marked the Hebrews' release from Egyptian slavery. God gave very specific instructions; at twilight, each family had to sacrifice a one year old, blemish free lamb, and then place its blood on the sides and tops of the doorframe of their house. Next, they were to roast it and eat it that evening with unleavened bread and bitter herbs. They were instructed to eat with their belts tied around their waist, sandals on their feet, and staff in their hand, so that they could be prepared to leave quickly (Exodus 12:1-13).

**New Testament Parallel:**
1. Jesus was the Lamb without blemish. He was crucified during the Passover Festival (Mark 14:1,12; 1 Peter 1:19).
2. The death of Christ marks our release from the slavery of sin. (Romans 8:2)

# FEAST OF UNLEAVENED BREAD (v6-8)

This was seven days of celebration to mark the exodus from Egypt. It was a reminder to the people that they were leaving the old life behind and entering a new way of living. Leaven was symbolic of decay or sin. This immediately followed Passover and involved removing all the leaven from the home.

**New Testament Parallel:**
1. Jesus the Messiah was sinless. He cleanses us from sin and imparts righteousness to us (Hebrews 4:15).
2. His body was in the grave during the first days of this feast (Mark 14:1,12 and Mark 15:42-46).
3. His body, the bread, broken for us (Mark 14:22).

## FEAST OF FIRST FRUITS (v9-14)

This was a one day celebration of the first crops of the barley harvest. It was a reminder to the people of God's provision.

**New Testament Parallel:**
1. Jesus's resurrection happened on this day (Mark 16:6 and 1 Corinthians 15:20).
2. He is our provision.

## FESTIVAL OF WEEKS/ PENTECOST (v19)

This was a one day celebration that commemorated the end of the barley harvest and the beginning of the wheat harvest. This is also celebrated as the remembrance of when God gave Moses and thus the Israelites the Torah as their guidance for how to live a holy life. This feast took place 50 days after the beginning of the Feast of Unleavened bread. It's a celebration of joy and thanksgiving for the bountiful harvest. For Christians today, it's a celebration of the giving of the Holy Spirit.

**New Testament Parallel:**
1. The Christian church was established on the day of Pentecost when the promised Helper, the Holy Spirit; filled the place Jesus had instructed His apostles and others, to go and wait (Acts 1:4-14). The Holy Spirit came in like a wind and tongues of fire rested on the heads of those who were present (Acts 2:1-4).
2. This points to the harvest of souls and the gift of the Holy Spirit for both Jews and Gentiles (Acts 10:44-48).

# FEAST OF TRUMPETS (v24)

This was a one day feast. It was the first of the Fall feasts that commemorated the beginning of the seventh month. It's also referred to as "Rosh-Hashanah" or "Jewish New Year." The celebration includes the blowing of the shofar and is celebrated to express joy and thanksgiving to God for a new year with the central theme being one of repentance and preparation for what is to come.

**New Testament Parallel:**
The return of the Messiah for His bride is always associated with the blowing of a loud trumpet. (1Thessalonians 4:13-18, 1Corinthians 15:52)

## DAY OF ATONEMENT (v27)

This was a one day celebration for the removal of sin from the people and the nation. During this time the priest would go into the Holy of Holies to make atonement for the sins of the people. The Day of Atonement, also known as "Yom Kippur," is a time of fasting, prayer, repentance, and reconciliation with God. It's a celebration of restored fellowship with God.

**New Testament Parallel:**
1. Jesus, the High Priest, died in our place. He paid the penalty of sin making atonement for us. (Hebrews 5:1-11 and Hebrews 7:11-19)
2. There are no further reparations to be made. It is finished!
3. Because of Jesus we can be reconciled to God once and for all!

## FEAST OF TABERNACLES (otherwise known as) FESTIVAL OF BOOTHS (v34)

This was a seven day festival commemorating God's protection and guidance as the Israelites traveled through the wilderness and lived in temporary shelters or tents, also called booths. It was celebrated about 6 months after Passover to renew Israel's commitment to God and trust in His guidance and protection.

**New Testament Parallel:**
Many scholars believe that this feast day prophetically points to the Lord's promise that He will once again tabernacle with His people when He returns to reign over all the world (Micah 4:1-7).

God is ever present with us! He will never leave us nor forsake us! We are His people.

As we read through the feasts, we see that the four Springtime feasts (Passover, Feast of Unleavened Bread, Feast of First Fruits, and Pentecost) were fulfilled on the actual feast day in connection with Christ's first coming. The three Fall feasts (Feast of Trumpets, Day of Atonement, and Feast of Tabernacles) are believed to be connected to Christ's second coming.

After reviewing the feasts, we quickly realize that God was very serious about the costliness of sin, and Jesus was the ultimate sacrifice. Thankfully, we don't have to go through these rituals any longer, we simply need to receive Christ and repent of our sin.

Of utmost significance and the primary focus of the feasts was the handling of blood. The blood of Christ is imperative because apart from it, we are separated from reconciliation with God and eternal life in heaven. There is power in the blood of Jesus because He has delivered us from the power of sin, which is eternal separation from God.

Colossians 1:13-14

*He has delivered us from the power of darkness and conveyed us into the kingdom of the Son of His love in whom we have redemption through His blood, the forgiveness of sins.*

Use this space below to share some of your own thoughts about what you learned about the Feasts.

Revelation 12:10-11

*"Then I heard a loud voice saying in Heaven, "now salvation, and strength, and the kingdom of our God, and the power of His Christ have come, for the accuser of our brethren, who accused them before our God day and night, has been cast down. And they overcame him by the blood of the Lamb and by the word of their testimony, and they did not love their lives to the death."*

The blood of Jesus and sharing our testimonies is what overcomes the enemy.

## NOTES:

BECAUSE

# CHAPTER 5

# UNITY

Ephesians 2:14-18
*For He himself is our peace, who has made both one, and has broken down the middle wall of separation, having abolished in His flesh the enmity, that is the law of commandments contained in ordinances, so as to create in Himself one new man from the two, thus making peace, and that He might reconcile them both to God in one body through the cross, thereby putting to death the enmity. And He came and preached peace to you who were afar off and to those who were near. For through Him we both have access by one Spirit to the Father.*

**Enmity:**
The Latin word for enemy is *inimicus*. From that word comes the word enmity, which is synonymous with animosity or hatred. Hostility and ill will are signs of enmity. It separates groups of people. We have seen this take place in politics, gender, race, and so much more. Dare I say "2020!" If that year taught us nothing else, it taught us that enmity divides! We live in a world of conflict that isn't much different than it was in Biblical times; it's just modernized now. Walls

of separation continue to divide us through social media, news outlets and other perceived normalities. Jesus broke down the walls of separation then, and He is our only hope for breaking down those walls now! Christ is our mediator. We must be reconciled to Him!

In Jesus' day; the Jews thought that their faith and traditions elevated them above everyone else. They considered anyone who was not a Jew to be beyond God's saving power, thus rendering any non-Jew ceremonially unclean and without hope. Because of how they were treated, the Gentiles resented the Jewish people, as well as their religious beliefs. Christ revealed both Jews and Gentiles were unclean before God. The only way they could become clean was through believing that Jesus was who He said He was.

## **Pride:**

The Jewish religious leaders; otherwise known as the Pharisees and Sadducees, were more concerned over their physical appearance of righteousness rather than righteousness itself. They enjoyed the attention they were given for the way they conducted themselves in prayer and their study of God's law. They thought they could gain God's approval just by memorizing and attempting to fulfill the letter of the law.

The Pharisees added their own man made rules to the law, thus putting demands on people God never intended. They even enforced them as though they held the same weight. If anyone violated their man-made rules, they were punished as though they violated the word of God itself. The Pharisees were <u>prideful</u>. Jesus and His disciples often clashed with these religious leaders.

**<u>Read Matthew 12:1-8</u>**

What day was being celebrated?

What were the disciples being accused of?

What reference did Jesus make ?

**<u>Read Matthew 12:9-14</u>**

What was Jesus doing that the Pharisees complained about?

## Read Luke 11:37-53

In the space below write out how Jesus describes the Pharisees, Scribes and Lawyers.

## Hypocrisy:

In Luke 12:1-3 Jesus warns His disciples to beware of the leaven of the Pharisees, which is hypocrisy. We previously discussed that "leaven" means decay or sin. Jesus goes on to say that there is nothing covered that will not be revealed, and whatever is spoken in the dark will be heard in the light and what is spoken in the inner room will be proclaimed on the housetops. That's some pretty strong language for how our Heavenly Father feels about hypocrisy!

Trying to appear good when our hearts are far from God is not to be taken lightly. Just as the Pharisees were eventually exposed and had to stand accountable for their selfishness and pride, so will we.

Read the parable of the Pharisee and the Tax collector found in Luke 18: 9-14.

Has there been a time in your life when you needed to be humbled? In the space provided describe what this verse teaches about humbleness before the Lord?

God used both the governing and religious leaders of the day to fulfill His plan and purpose. The Pharisees arrested Jesus. He was put on trial by the Sanhedrin, the highest ruling council of the Jews, and eventually sentenced to death by Pontius Pilate, the Governor of Judaea.

Jesus fulfilled the "Law" once and for all. Matthew 5:17 is clear on His purpose "Do not think that I came to destroy the Law or the Prophets. I did not come to destroy but to fulfill." Because of Christ's life, death and resurrection we have been granted new life without the restrictions of the Law (Galatians 3).

When we accept Jesus as Lord and Savior of our life, we have the promise of John 3:16. Jesus came that we all may have salvation. He came that we will have life in heaven eternally with Him and not be separated from Him. Isaiah prophesied "by His stripes we are healed." That healing relates to being healed from eternal condemnation (Isaiah 53:5).

## Salvation:

The promise of salvation is certain for all who believe in the name of Jesus. Everyone who calls on the name of the Lord will be saved (Acts 2:21).

Because we are His children, we are held accountable by God, our Father, to do what He says. We don't get to live anyway we want to without accountability. As a child of the King of Kings, we are held to a higher standard. It is our responsibility to be about our Father's business and represent Him well in the earth (Matthew 6:10).

Jesus is concerned with how we treat others and how we represent Him. In Matthew 7:21-26 He says *"not everyone who says to Me Lord, Lord, shall enter the kingdom of heaven but he who does the will of My Father in heaven. Many will say to Me in the day,"Lord, Lord, have we not prophesied in Your name, cast out demons in Your name and done many wonders in Your name? And then I will declare to them,"I never knew you, depart from Me you who practice lawlessness!" Therefore whoever hears these sayings of Mine and does them, I will liken him to a wise man who built his house on the rock; and the rain descended, the floods came, and the winds blew and beat on that house; and it did not fall, for it was founded on the rock. But everyone who hears these sayings of Mine and does not do them, will be like a foolish man who built his house on the sand; and the rain descended, the floods came, and the winds blew and beat on that house; and it fell and great was its fall."*

Write out the responsibility required according to the following scripture verses.

1. Hebrews 12:14

2. 1 John 4:7

3. 1 Thessalonians 5:15

4. Romans 12:8

5. Matthew 12:36

Psalm 11:5
*The Lord tests the righteous, but the wicked and the one who loves violence His soul hates.*

God hates sin, but thanks to Christ's death and resurrection we are set free from the penalty of sin. Enmity no longer exists. Christ has destroyed prejudice and other sinful barriers we put between us. His work on the cross allows us to have reconciliation with Him and unity with one another. Jesus was speaking to His disciples when He said these words found in John 13:35 "By this all will know that you are my disciples, if you have love for one another."

Take a few moments to pray this prayer with me:
*"Lord Jesus, I invite you to show me the areas in my heart that are hindering the work you want to do through me. Forgive me for any offense I may be holding on to. Speak to me as only you can. Do what only you can. I surrender to You, Your plan and Your will. Give me the opportunity and the words I need to speak to be reconciled with my brothers and sisters.*
*In Jesus Name- Amen"*

## **Forgiveness:**
Reconciliation is not easy and neither is forgiveness. However, forgiveness is humbling for both the one being forgiven and the forgiver. Forgiving someone

doesn't mean that all of a sudden we are a-okay with what our offender did, and it doesn't instantaneously take the pain away. However, what it does do is take away a burden that we were never meant to carry ourselves in the first place. It's acknowledging to the offender "Christ forgave me and therefore I forgive you." When we forgive, we are admitting that we are not a judge or jury, and we release them from the bondage we have held over them. In addition, we also release ourselves from the bondage that unforgiveness has on us. It's a win-win situation. "All have sinned and fallen short of the glory of God *(Romans3:23)."* Our justification, or being made righteous in Christ, can happen only through the redemptive blood of Jesus Christ shed on the cross at Calvary. Jesus understood the power of forgiveness. We move toward unity and reconciliation when we humble ourselves and forgive those who have hurt us.

Romans 12:3
*For I say, through the grace given me, to everyone who is among you, not to think of himself more highly than he ought to think, but to think soberly, as God has dealt to each one a measure of faith.*

When we humble ourselves and look at one another as image bearers of Christ we can move away from

the things that divide us. We can move toward reconciliation; forgive one another and allow the Holy Spirit to do the work in us that will ultimately lead us to unity.
Below I've listed a few ideas for how to create unity.

- Focus on the mission at hand
- Submit willingly to each other
- Allow each person to operate in their calling and authority.
- Understand the value each person brings

What are some other ways you can create unity? Write them out below for each area.

Family:


Church:


Work:


Neighborhood:

# BECAUSE

# CHAPTER 6

# ADOPTED

The dictionary defines adoption as "the action or act of legally taking another's child and bringing him/her up as one's own."

There's a name exchange that takes place in adoption. An amended birth certificate is issued, replacing the biological parents with the adopting parents' names and the child's new name.

The adopted child will then be brought up according to the ways of his/her new family as though they were born into it naturally. They will be entitled to all the privileges that come with being part of the family unit. They will take part in family traditions; sit at the table for family dinner; and develop patterns of behavior and security as their needs are met, all while they are being nurtured, educated, loved, cared for and protected. Part of their protection will be in the form of family rules, guidelines, and boundaries. They are representatives of their new family unit and will be expected to represent well. Likewise; God does the same for us. Once we accept Him as our heavenly Father, we are brought into a His family and given a new name. We now represent Him.

He determined in advance (predestined) that:
- He would adopt us as His sons and daughters (Ephesians 1:5).
- He chose our home for us (John 14:2-4).
- He waits for us (Isaiah 30:18).
- Our citizenship belongs to Heaven (Philippians 3:20).

Ephesians 1:4-5
*Blessed be the God and Father of our Lord Jesus Christ, who has blessed us with every spiritual blessing in the heavenly places in Christ, just as He chose us in Him before the foundation of the world, that we should be holy and without blame before Him in love, having predestined us to adoption as sons by Jesus Christ to Himself, according to the good pleasure of His will, to the praise of the glory of His grace, by which He made us accepted in the Beloved.*

Take a few minutes to ponder the words of Ephesians 1:4-5 and write your thoughts below about how it makes you feel to know God **chose** you.

When we allow God to be the Father of our lives we are given the name " Adopted son/daughter, holy and without blame." We are no longer a son or daughter of Adam carrying the name "Shameful" or "Blemished." Our names have been changed to "Forgiven, Shameless, Blameless, Justified." We are loved by God Almighty! We call Him Abba Father out of deep reverence and admiration for who He is and what He has done for us through Jesus the Christ.

John 3:16-17
*For God so loved the world that He gave His only begotten Son that whoever believes in Him should not perish but have everlasting life. For God did not send His Son into the world to condemn the world, but that the world through Him might be saved.*

There is absolutely no human on the planet that Jesus did not give His life for, and the first step to everlasting life in heaven is to believe Jesus exists! Second, we must believe He is who He says He is, and that He came to do what He said He came to do.

**<u>Read John 6:26-29</u>**

What does Jesus say is the work of God?

God doesn't want to condemn anyone, and He won't coerce us into believing in Him. We must choose to believe of our own free will. When we believe in name of Jesus and repent of our sins, we are adopted into the Royal Family of the King of Kings and Lord of Lords.

Colossians 2:6-7
*As you therefore have received Christ Jesus the Lord, so walk in Him, rooted and built up in Him and established in the faith, as you have been taught, abounding in it with Thanksgiving.*

Just as God wanted the offerings we read about in the Old Testament to be willingly given; He wants us completely submit to Him of our own free will, not because of what He does, but because of Who He is. When we make it a daily practice to study and pray His word, we bring honor to our heavenly Father. We are showing Him that what He has to say is important to us. If we choose not to repent and not turn away from sin, we hinder our relationship with Him.

Malachi 1:6
*"A son honors his father, And a servant his master. If then I am the Father, Where is My honor? And if I am a Master, Where is My reverence?" Says the LORD of hosts.*

Take a minute to contemplate God as your Father, What does it mean to you to be His child?

Most certainly, there are benefits to being a child of God! However, when we focus only on the benefits of what God gives, rather than honoring Him for **Who** He is, we miss the point! The Bible speaks very highly of honor! We should honor God because the position of Father is an honorable position!

So what does that mean to us? It means that we make a conscious choice to no longer participate in things that hinder our relationship with Him. Anything in our lives contrary to God's word has to go.

Ephesians 4:21-24
*If indeed you have heard Him and have been taught by Him, as the truth is in Jesus: that you put off, concerning your former conduct, the old man which grows corrupt according to the deceitful lusts, and be renewed in the spirit of your mind, and that you put on the new man which was created according to God, in true righteousness and holiness.*

In other words, it's our responsibility to repent, turn away from and not return to those things that God's word says are not good.

Read Ephesians 4:25-32 and fill in the blanks.

Put away _____ and speak truth to your neighbor

Be Angry but do not_____

Do not let the sun go down on your_____
Do not give place to the devil.

If you steal_____

Work with your hands that which is _____

Give to someone in need

Let no corrupt word proceed from your_____

Because we are adopted through the blood of Jesus into the family of God we have expectations to live up too. God expects that we honor and revere Him as Father, but we are also to honor and respect one another. Because we are all created in His image

*(Genesis 1:26)*, we are held accountable for our actions toward other image bearers of Christ. As God's children, we are to be kind, tenderhearted and forgive because Christ forgave us. There is no workaround for this. No matter how much sense our point of view makes to us, regardless of how right we are, we can lose our effectiveness if we are not courteous and respectful to others. It will serve us well to remember "Who" we represent.

In the space provided below write out a few ways you can better represent Christ today.

BECAUSE

# CHAPTER 7

# PRAYER

The greatest privilege given to us is the opportunity to speak with our heavenly Father whenever we want. It is through prayer that we overcome the everyday challenges of life. He promises that He is our ever present help in time of trouble (Psalm 46:1). He delights and rejoices in us (Isaiah 62:4). He invites us to ask Him for what we need (Matthew 7:7). I have heard people say, "I don't know how to pray or what to pray for." That's okay! God will hear a simple "God Help" just as He will hear a longer prayer. Jesus gave us an outline for how to pray. We can see it in Matthew 6:9-13 and also in Luke 11:2-4.

## "The Lord's Prayer"

*Our Father, in heaven, hallowed be Your name; Your kingdom come; Your will be done on earth as it is in heaven. Give us this day our daily bread; and forgive us our debts, as we forgive our debtors And do not lead us into temptation, but deliver us from the evil one. For Yours is the kingdom and the power and the glory forever. Amen*

This is a wonderful prayer to memorize and pray regularly, but we should be cautious that it doesn't lose its meaning through habitual recitation. Take some time to think about the importance of these words.

- **_Our Father_**
    - Our relationship is established-we acknowledge who He is and that we belong to Him
    - We know we can come to Him in confidence
    - We know we can trust Him
    - We know He loves us
- **_Hallowed_**
    - He is Holy
    - He is praiseworthy
    - He deserves honor
- **_Your Name-Your Kingdom- Your Will_**
    - Recognition of His Sovereignty
    - His supreme power and authority
    - Our surrender
- **_Give us our daily bread_**
    - Our daily provision comes from Him
    - We ask with humble dependence
- **_Forgiveness_**
    - We recognize that we have sinned and ask for forgiveness
    - Our forgiveness is from Him alone
    - We must forgive others

- ***Temptation***
  - My own carelessness and disobedience
  - My natural (fleshly) bent for that which is wrong or unwise
- ***Deliver us***
  - Protection
  - Rescue

Recognizing the Sovereignty of God is our first step to answered prayer. The second step is understanding that "Yes", "No", and "Not Yet" are complete answers, and because He is sovereign, He doesn't owe us an explanation. God is always working in our favor whether we realize it or not.

"Because I said so" may not sit well with us, but we can rest in knowing that God's "Because I said so" has a heavenly purpose. Ephesians 3:20 tells us that He can do exceedingly above anything we could think or imagine. If we could understand everything in our human minds, He wouldn't be a very big God, now would He? He is not a puny being.

### *Does that mean we shouldn't bother praying?*
No it does not. 1 Thessalonians 5:17 tells us to pray without ceasing. Our job is to trust in Him with all our heart and lean not on our own understanding (Proverbs 3:5).

### *Is that easy to just accept?*
Not always but we aren't promised easy. Psalm 34:19 tells us many are the afflictions of the righteous. But the Lord is with us through every one of them. We may not always get what we want but we will get what we need. God is always for us (Romans 8:31). His character and His intentions are pure.

### *Does God get mad when we are angry and complain about His decisions?*
Sometimes! Scripture has many stories where God's anger was aroused. Here are a few.

- Read Numbers 14:1-12
- Read Numbers 22:22-34
- Read Matthew 21:12-13

### *Does God change His mind?*
I really struggled with how to answer this question because to answer "Yes" would indicate a deficiency in the mind of God, and since God is perfect, He needs no improvement.

Isaiah 55:8-9 tells us that His thoughts and His ways are not the same as ours. We are limited by our human understanding. We may change our minds from one thing to another depending on our current circumstances or the outcome we want. For example,

I change my mind about what I want to wear; or what I want to eat, or what I want to do, or any number of things depending on how I feel. At times, if I see a better way to do something, I will change my mind to do it differently. God knows all things beginning to end. He has no limitations. His capacity is of a completely different level than our human capacity. We are human; we are going to fail. We may even have doubts and grumble or complain, but through Jesus we have hope and redemption. We have a Father who is ready to forgive us. He shows us mercy and grace in spite of ourselves. He has a plan for our lives and promises to guide us in it. We are never alone, even if we feel differently. God always answers prayer.

Let's take a look at a few "Yes," "No," and "Not yet" answers we find in scripture:

## **"YES"**
## **Read 1 Samuel 1:9-20**
- Who was praying?


- What did she ask?


- How did God answer?

## Read Mark 10: 46-52
- Who cried out for help?

- What did he ask?

- What did Jesus do?

## "NO"
## Read Deuteronomy 3:23-29
- Who was pleading with the Lord?

- What did he ask?

- What did God answer?

## Read Luke 22:41-44
- Who was praying?

- What did He ask?

- What was the outcome?

## "NOT YET"
## Read 1 Kings 18:41-45
- Who was praying?

- What did He pray?

- How many times did the servant go to look?

- What was the response?

## Read John 11:32-44
- What did Jesus pray?

- What was the outcome?

We would probably be a lot less frustrated if we remember that what *we think* we need, and what *God knows* we need, are often quite different. Bottom line is He will always supply our needs. His word tells us that His ways are not our ways and His thoughts are not our thoughts (Isaiah 55:8-9). It's not our job to figure it out. It's our job to trust Him because He is God and He is good.

The earth we live in was called "good" by the Creator and when sin entered, decay started both physically and spiritually. This side of heaven there will be a lot of "Why God" moments. Many of which we may never have an answer for. We can't sugar coat it. Life is hard and sometimes it just doesn't seem fair or logical to us that a good God would allow bad things to happen to good people. But when we know God's character, we can trust that even in sickness, struggle, sorrow and anything else we go through- God doesn't waste a thing. He is Sovereign!

Throughout history we see time and again how the Lord turned something horrible into something beautiful. Paul's life is an example of that. The Samaritan woman, Lazarus, Joseph, Mary, David, Ruth and countless others we read about in the Bible are all good examples, but the greatest of all is Jesus's work on the cross.

Take a moment and reflect on how God took something you went through and turned it into something beautiful. Write it out in the space below and/or share it with the group.

BECAUSE

# CHAPTER 8

# INTERCESSION AND FASTING

When we are in a relationship with someone we love, we will communicate with them regularly, and talk to them about anything, and everything that we deem important. Prayer is our communication with God; it's our worship and our praise. We pour out our hearts before Him; believing in Him, His word, and trusting that He hears us and will answer us. We believe that He will do what we ask; but we trust above all else, that He will answer in the way that He sees most fit. In prayer, we share our hearts deepest desires through the help of the Holy Spirit. Intercession is different from regular prayer in that; when we intercede for someone else, we are taking on their need as though it were our own. We willingly sacrifice our own agenda, time, passion and desire for someone else's benefit. We stand in their shoes.

The Greek word for intercession is *"Enteuxis"- a meeting with; then, a conversation; consequently, a petition to a king on behalf of someone else.*
In other words, we are **boldly** approaching the Lord, **petitioning** Him on behalf of someone else. We are

**standing** in the gap between that person and God with **powerful fervor** from the Holy Spirit within us. Intercessory prayers are spiritually forceful; impactful prayers that are unyielding and tenacious. Intercession has the power to change the course, destiny and future history of nations. We see examples of this in the Bible.

## Read Numbers 14:1-9

Why are the Israelites grumbling?

Who are they grumbling against?

## Read Numbers 14: 10-20

What was God's first response to their grumbling?

In v12 what did He say He would do?

In v13 we see Moses begin to intercede on behalf of the Israelites, what does he say could happen if God killed them all off and disinherited them?

As a result of Moses' prayer, God pardoned the Israelites (v20), but they still had the consequences of their actions to contend with.

**Read Numbers 14:21-24**

What were the consequences?

What was God's promise towards Caleb and why?

**Read Romans 8:26-27**

Who helps us in our weakness?

When we don't know what to pray, what does the Spirit do on our behalf?

**Read Romans 8:31-34**

What stands out to you in these verses?

It's both humbling and comforting to know that Jesus and the Holy Spirit intercede on our behalf. I can't think of a better tag team to have in my corner.

## Fasting

Fasting is abstaining from food for an allotted time while focusing on prayer, God's word, and drawing closer to Him. Fasting gives more emphasis on prayer because rather than feeding our physical bodies the things that are pleasing to us; we are exhibiting a hunger for the things that are pleasing to Him; thus deepening our relationship with Him and enabling us to do what He desires.

1. Fasting increases our faith; without it we aren't able to move and operate effectively.

    **Read Matthew 17:14-20**

What were the disciples unable to do?

What did Jesus say was the reason?

2. Fasting puts the focus on what matters; when it's combined with intercession, it compels the heart of God.

   ### Read Nehemiah 1:1-11

   How did Nehemiah address God?

   What was Nehemiah reminding God of?

   What was he asking God for?

   What did he confess on behalf of all the people?

   What did he recall about the promises of God?

3. Fasting increases our ability to hear instruction from the Lord; for the benefit of others, and ourselves.

   ### Read Exodus 34:28

BECAUSE

What was the end result of Moses' fasting?

4. Fasting strengthens us for service and withstanding the temptations and attacks of the enemy.

### **Read Matthew 4:1-11**

What stands out to you in these scripture verses?

## **Fasting Preparation:**

### **Read Matthew 6:16-18**

List out the steps to take in preparation for fasting?

You may already know of someone you can intercede for by prayer and fasting. Perhaps you have a family member or friend that is going through a difficult time and really needs to hear from the Lord. It could be someone who isn't even in a relationship with the Lord yet, but you feel an unction from the Holy Spirit to pray for them. If you can't think of anyone, ask God to place someone on your heart to pray for. Ask the Holy Spirit to guide you in how to pray specifically for that person. Press in and believe!

Here are a few ideas to get you started.
- Missionaries
- Country
- Pastors
- Church
- Souls
- Community

Learn what you can about the specific person or group you will represent. For example, if you are interceding for a missionary in Africa; take some time to learn about the area where they are living and the people they are ministering to. In your community; take a walk around your neighborhood and ask the Holy Spirit to show you which home He wants you to pray for.

BECAUSE

# CHAPTER 9

# SPIRITUAL UNDERSTANDING

Proverbs 2:6:
*For the Lord gives wisdom; from his mouth come knowledge and understanding.*

Spiritual understanding is the ability to understand and grow in the knowledge of Jesus through Bible study, prayer, reading God's word and seeking Godly counsel. It's what you are doing now; learning about the Lord in a more intimate way. Let's face it, this side of heaven we can't possibly learn everything there is about Him. Our human minds can't comprehend it; it's indescribable, but the joy and the excitement of discovering who He is and how very much He loves us is indispensable.

Paul had great compassion for the churches he encouraged. He prayed on their behalf to increase in knowledge and understanding so that they could bear good fruit and be fully pleasing to Him.

## **Read Colossians 1:9-23**

Paul tells us that by seeking understanding; the church would be strengthened in their faith, well grounded, steadfast and not moved away from the hope of the gospel.

In your own words, write out a prayer using Colossians 1:9-11.




When we understand why we believe something we tend to not get swayed by counterfeit truth. This is why studying the word of God is vital in our walk with Him.

God's word is our offense weapon (Ephesians 6:17). In His word, God counsels and makes promises of what will ensue from our response to that counsel. I often refer to this as God's "If/Then" statements. Perhaps in childhood you heard something similar to this from your parents; *"If you clean up your room, then you can play with your friends."* The "If" was the counsel.

The "Then" was the result that would follow. Hopefully you chose wisely.

King Solomon, the wisest man who ever lived (1 Kings 3:12), is credited with writing most of Proverbs which is a book full of godly wisdom he personally gained throughout his life. Let's take a look at what he has to say.

**Read Proverbs 2:1-22**

In the excerpt from v1-5 below, put a circle around "if" and underline "then"

My son, if you accept my words and store up my commands within you, turning your ear to wisdom and applying your heart to understanding, indeed, if you call out for insight and cry aloud for understanding and if you look for it as silver and search for it as for hidden treasure, then you will understand the fear of the Lord and find the knowledge of God.

Apply the text you read to the following.

v2 Where should we turn our ear?

## BECAUSE

v3 What should we apply our heart to?

v5 What is the promise of accepting God's words and storing up His commands?

v6 Who gives wisdom?

v10-11 What happens when wisdom enters our heart?

v12-v16 List out the things wisdom will save you from.

v22 What will happen to the wicked and unfaithful?

Hebrews 4:12

*For the word of God is living and powerful, and sharper than any two-edged sword, piercing even to the division of soul and spirit, and of joints and marrow, and is a discerner of the thoughts and intents of the heart.*

The old saying "sticks and stones may break my bones, but your words will never hurt me" is a bold faced lie! Our words do matter! Careless words have the potential to cause damage that can take years to repair and for some, it may be irreparable. We should speak life to those around us.

When we know what the word says and follow Jesus's example by speaking "IT IS WRITTEN," it delivers a deathblow to the enemy of our soul.

Previously, in Matthew 4:1-11; we read how Jesus used the power of the word to combat against the temptations from the enemy. Satan is so prideful that he had the audacity to think that the very Son of God could be foiled by his schemes. The Bible warns us that Satan is very crafty, and walks around like a prowling lion to see who he can devour (1 Peter 5:8). He will attack when we are at our most vulnerable state, and he will attack when we think we have it all together. Often, he will tempt us with the things that appeal to our humanness.

- Our physical state
- Our influence
- Our Self-worth

But, when we understand the power of speaking the word of God, we can resist him, and he will flee from us (James 4:7).

Take a few minutes and ask God to show you where you are most vulnerable. Use the space to write out what the Holy Spirit reveals to you.

My physical state:

My influence:

My self-worth:

Now let's get battle ready. Read the scriptures below. In the space provided, write out what you find for each one. I've completed the first one as an example.

## **Physical state:**

Isaiah 41:10
- *My God is with me*
- *I am His*
- *He will strengthen me*
- *He will help me*
- *He will uphold me*


1 Corinthians 6:20

## **Mental state:**

John 14:27

Philippians 4:8-9

## **Influence:**

2 Timothy 2:14-16

2 Corinthians 6:14-18

## **Self worth:**

2 Timothy 1:7

Hebrews 13:6

1 Peter 1:13-16

*Therefore gird up the loins of your mind, be sober, and rest your hope fully upon the grace that is to be brought to you at the revelation of Jesus Christ; as obedient children, not conforming yourselves to the former lusts, as in your ignorance; but as He who called you is holy, you also be holy in all your conduct, because it is written, "Be holy, for I am holy."*

Our plan for righteous living:

- Prepare for action, get ready for hard work, get ready for battle, be disciplined -*Gird up the loins of your mind*
- Stay Focused, have sound thoughts, be precise, clear and unwavering - *sober*
- Be obedient children of God
- Practice holiness -*holy in all our conduct, not conforming to the ways of our past sins*

Take some time in prayer asking God to show you areas of disobedience in your life and reveal to you how to be holy.

# BECAUSE

# CHAPTER 10

# DISCIPLESHIP AND THE GREAT COMMISSION

Simply stated; a "disciple" is a follower of Christ; and "discipleship" is the action of learning and producing Christ-like character. It really boils down to practicing discipline, which is defined as training oneself for a particular behavior or outcome. If our desire is to be more like Christ; then we must practice living a Christ-like life.

Christian Disciplines have been established to help us do just that; become better disciples by developing and training ourselves, and others; to grow in our relationships with the Lord.

I don't think there is a specific list designated in scripture called *"The Bible list of Disciplines."* However, there have been many books written in regard to the disciplines of Christianity that are Biblically based. You may want to look for books on this topic at your local library or your favorite book store if you are interested in learning more. Below, I've listed several disciplines that are evident within the Bible and therefore relevant to us for putting into practice.

- Prayer
- Bible Study
- Fasting
- Worship
- Rest
- Discipleship
- Service(ministry to others)
- Tithing

**<u>Read Romans 10:14-15</u>**

What was Paul's concern about the Gospel?



If you have ever felt intimidated by the concept of telling someone about Jesus and leading them through the steps to salvation, I have some good news for you, the word of God does it for us! All we need to do is let it- BECAUSE- It is Written!!

Here is an example of what is commonly referred to as The Roman Road to Salvation:

***Romans 3:23-*** *for all have sinned and fall short of the glory of God*

***Romans 5:8-*** *But God demonstrates His own love toward us, in that while we were still sinners, Christ died for us*

***Romans 10:9-*** *That if you confess with your mouth the Lord Jesus and believe in your heart that God has raised Him from the dead, you will be saved*

***Romans 10:13-*** *For "whoever calls on the name of the Lord shall be saved"*

***Romans 8:1-*** *There is therefore now no condemnation to those who are in Christ Jesus, who do not walk according to the flesh, but according to the spirit.*

The salvation message can be shared in simple ways too:

## **COLORS:**

**Black-** Our sin separates us from God.

**Red** - Jesus paid the penalty for sin by dying on the cross.

**White**-When we repent of our sins, we are made clean.

**Green**- Grow closer to God.

**Yellow-** Eternal life with Jesus.

## ABC's:
**A**dmit- I am a sinner.
**B**elieve-I believe Jesus died for me.
**C**onfess- I confess He is my Lord.

## THREE R's
**R**ecognize- I recognize I am a sinner.
**R**epent- I repent of my sin.
**R**eceive- I receive Jesus my Lord and Savior.

# The Great Commission

## Read Matthew 28:16-20

What does Jesus tell the disciples to do?

Where are they to go?

What are they to do when they get there?

**GO**-simply put, don't stay where you are; grow in Christ, and share your testimony with others. Some people are called to missions, while others are given the means to send those who are called. If you've never been on a mission trip, I encourage you to go. I think too often we try to complicate missions. Not everyone can travel, and not everyone has the means to send others, but one thing everyone can do is PRAY! Pray for those who are in other countries, and pray for those who are participating in local missions. We all have a part to play in spreading the Gospel of Jesus Christ. What we don't have, is an excuse for doing absolutely nothing.

**BAPTIZE**- comes from the greek word *"baptiso"* which means "to immerse." Baptism is an outward confession of an inward faith. When we are baptized, we are stating "Jesus is Lord of my life, I believe He came; I believe He died; I believe He rose again; and I believe He is coming back for me someday. Until then I proclaim He is in control, I have repented and I am made clean. My sin is washed away."

**DISCIPLE-** verb-*teach*; noun-*student, pupil*- Being a new creation in Christ doesn't mean everything will be perfect and we won't have any difficulty. As a matter of fact, the enemy will do everything he can to discourage someone new in the faith. This is why it's vitally important we build a community that is beneficial for new believers to grow spiritually and not criticize them for what they do not know. We want to assist them along the way, by encouraging them and teaching them about the things of the Lord. We need to be willing and able to answer the "why" questions they have. As Christian men and women, it is our privilege to help others walk out the Christian life and guide them along the way. We must lead by example!

## Read Matthew 13:1-9

What can we do to help someone cultivate in good soil?




## Read 1 Timothy 1:1-11

Paul's letter to Timothy was written during his time on death row in a Roman prison. He was about to be executed for preaching and teaching the Gospel, but that did not prevent him from encouraging Timothy to continue in the ministry regardless of opposition and persecution. Paul lived by example, even from a jail cell. He trusted Timothy to hold the leaders accountable. False teaching had begun to creep into the church because many who desired to teach, did not have the correct understanding of what they were saying, and as a result, they were misleading their parishioners. Discipleship is something that has to be taught verbally and by example. The leaders had to be prepared to teach others so they could in turn share the message and spread it through the nations. The Gospel message was the main thing and anything added to or taken away from it was a distraction that simply didn't belong in the church.

It was important to Paul that Timothy stayed where he was to ensure that the leaders were teaching correctly because those who were being lead had no formal understanding. The Gospel message is not for those who are righteous already, but for those who are unrighteous.

Use the space below to list out the people Paul says the Gospel message is for (v8-10).

Pray with me.
*Father God let our hearts be burdened for those who need to hear the Gospel message. In Jesus Name- Amen*

## **Read 2 Timothy 2:1-26**

Paul is clear that we shouldn't be arguing over unimportant details or have foolish discussions. There are some arguments we are never going to win. Some controversies are really just not that important and tend to divide the body of Christ rather than unite it.

Paul wanted the churches to have the tools they needed to develop disciples who could help spread the good news throughout the nations. As the churches grew, there were new hurdles to get over and new issues to address. He understood that Timothy would have many trials ahead, and he used his experience to disciple Timothy for that reason.

It's important for us to disciple one another and encourage one another to stand firm on what we believe, even when we are faced with persecution. What we go through is never wasted, it's our testimony. Our past experiences, whether good or bad, can be used as opportunities to help others. We are never beyond hope.

One of the keys to being a disciple is to be teachable. We have a lot to learn from one another. In closing I want you to ask yourself these two questions.

Are you being discipled?

Who can you disciple?

If you are being discipled already, that is wonderful news. Continue to lean in and learn all you can. Ask the Holy Spirit to give you a hunger for His word and His ways so that you can grow in your knowledge and understanding of Him. Then, ask Him to show you someone He wants you to disciple. If you are not being discipled yet, ask God to connect you with godly men and women who can disciple you. There may be a group within your local church you can get involved with, find out and sign up.

Is there someone within your circle of influence that you can disciple? Remember, it doesn't have to be within the 4 walls of your church; it could be in your neighborhood, work place, or even within your own family. Ask God to lay someone on your heart and give you the opportunity to disciple them for His purpose and His glory. Undoubtedly He will do it! BECAUSE- it is written!

# BECAUSE

# ABOUT THE AUTHOR

Michele and her husband Joel have been married for more than 30 years. She has served in many leadership roles within the church including women's ministry, young adults, and small groups. She has spoken at several retreats and churches around the Bay Area. BECAUSE is her second Bible study book and is written with new believers in mind. Her first Bible study book is entitled B.E.G.I.N. (**B**e **E**verything **G**od **I**ntended **N**ow)- this is an 8 week long small group study that covers 8 basic topics relevant for the church body including Physical and Spiritual health, Missions, Finances, Friendship, Servanthood, Organization, and Overcoming Fear. She is an advocate for those who want to learn more about Jesus and the purpose He has for them on the earth. She believes in the power of prayer and the undeniable work of the Holy Spirit to change our hearts and draw us to Him.

www.ingramcontent.com/pod-product-compliance
Lightning Source LLC
LaVergne TN
LVHW051747080426
835511LV00018B/3250